SHARKS
& UNDERWATER PREDATORS

SHARKS
& UNDERWATER PREDATORS

TOM JACKSON

This pocket edition first published in 2024

First published in 2020

Copyright © 2024 Amber Books Ltd

All rights reserved. No part of this publication may be reproduced, stored in a retrieval system, or transmitted in any form or by any means, electronic, mechanical, photocopying, recording, or otherwise, without prior written permission of the copyright holder.

Published by
Amber Books Ltd
United House
London N7 9DP
United Kingdom

www.amberbooks.co.uk
Facebook: amberbooks
YouTube: amberbooksltd
Instagram: amberbooksltd
X(Twitter): @amberbooks

ISBN: 978-1-83886-443-9

Project Editor: Anna Brownbridge
Designers: Keren Harragan and Andrew Easton
Picture Research: Terry Forshaw

Printed in China

Contents

Introduction	6
Galean Sharks	8
Dogfish and Bullhead Sharks	72
Rays & Skates	106
Other Predators	144
Marine Mammal Hunters	206
PICTURE CREDITS	224

Introduction

The shark is an animal one never forgets. Once we see its sleek, muscle-bound body and effortless ocean power in the water, we pay attention. Then there are the teeth: big, sharp and never in short supply. After that, all it takes for us to think, 'Shark!' is the merest glimpse of a triangular dorsal fin slicing through the surface of the sea.

Sharks, and their close relative the rays (armed with stingers and electric shockers), make an intriguing study of the many ways that marine predators can kill. Sharks have been plying their trade as top ocean predators for more than 400 million years. In that time, they have adapted in many ways. Today, the biggest sharks – and biggest fish – are harmless giants that sift food from the water instead of taking it by force, and smaller dogfish sharks are expert hunters of prey that crowd the twilight zones of the open ocean. Of course, while they dominate, sharks have no monopoly on hunting in the ocean. There are predators of all kinds, all colours and all sizes out there – from glittering jellyfish to gargantuan sperm whales.

ABOVE:
The blue-ringed octopus wants to be left alone – their characteristic blue and black rings change colour when they feel threatened. Its deadly venom can kill a person in minutes.

OPPOSITE:
One can never tell if we are watching a great white shark or whether it is watching us. Nevertheless, this monstrous shark needs our help as its population is steadily declining.

Galean Sharks

If you were to mentally picture a shark, the chances are high that your image would be of a galean species. This seldom-used term groups together the biggest and meanest of the sharks, which all share the same helmet-like skull structure (*galea* means 'helmet' in ancient Greek). There are around 300 species in this grouping, which is divided into three orders: ground sharks, mackerel sharks and carpet sharks.

Ground sharks, or Carcharhiniformes, make up the bulk of this group and are in fact the most numerous order of sharks of any kind. They include famed and familiar species such as the hammerhead shark, plus some scary foes, such as the tiger shark and bull shark. On top of that ground sharks include catsharks, which are small, slender bottom feeders. Bottom-feeding species are also well represented in the Orectolobiformes, or carpet sharks. Rather charmingly, these are named after the way their elaborate camouflage markings reminded naturalists of carpets – although the fashion for carpet designs has changed considerably since that time. The carpet sharks include the wobbegongs, nurse shark and the whale shark, which is the largest fish species of all.

The final galean order is the Lamniformes, or mackerel sharks. There are about 20 species in this order, and most have made their mark in the popular imagination. There is the porbeagle, which can appear almost friendly, the mako, basking shark, goblin shark, thresher shark and, above all, the great white.

OPPOSITE:
Shark silhouettes
A school of hammerhead sharks gathers off the Pacific coast of Mexico. Large groups of these big sharks gather here in summer to breed.

ALL PHOTOGRAPHS:
Hammerhead
These sharks, found in coastal waters worldwide, are unmistakable thanks to the cephalofoil, or hammer-shaped head. As well as providing some hydrodynamic benefits, the wing-like head is chiefly a detection system. The underside picks up electrical signals from the movement of prey, and the widely spread nostrils on either tip allow the shark to discern the direction of chemical scents in the water to a greater accuracy.

LEFT:
Tiger shark
Growing to 5m (16ft), this is one of the bigger and more dangerous species of predatory shark (to humans, that is). It lives in tropical waters around much of the world and has a famously catholic diet, including all kinds of sea life from sea snakes to dolphins.

ABOVE:
Sideways teeth
Tiger sharks have an unusual dentition. The teeth are serrated, with smaller saw-like edges, which is a common feature of shark teeth, but they also have a backwards slanted kink, creating a claw-like shape. The teeth are also shorter than is typical of a shark of this size, but still have sturdy roots. As a result, tiger shark teeth are able to slice and crack through any foods, even a turtle shell, while bigger-toothed species will often lose teeth when tackling this kind of tougher seafood.

Fish eye view

This uncomfortably close image shows the insides of a tiger shark's gaping mouth. The tiny pits on the snout are ampullae of Lorenzini. They are filled with electrolyte gel that picks up the tiny electric fields created by the nerves and muscles of animals. These electroreceptors guide the shark in for the killer strike, even through dark or muddy waters.

ABOVE:
Shark town
The fertile waters off South Africa's Cape of Good Hope are a haven for sea life of all kinds, and sharks are a common sight here.

OPPOSITE:
Shark attacks
The deadliest sharks roam the oceans and can attack anywhere outside of polar waters. However, attacks are most common around southern Africa, Australia and California, places where humans and sharks are more likely to meet. Yet, the statistics belie the perceived threats. In a typical year about 70 people are bitten by sharks of all kinds in unprovoked attacks and 6 of those die.

Blue shark
In the dark waters, this shark's pupil has opened wide. The blue shark is one of the requiem sharks. The root of this name is contested, and is probably not from the French term for 'resting', now used to describe funereal anthems. Instead, the modern name is probably a mangling of an old French term for 'baring the teeth'.

ABOVE:
Blue shark skin
This species is named for the blue shading of the upper body. The darker blues transition through streaks and blotches on the flanks to being a near-white on the belly.

RIGHT TOP:
Widespread hunter
The blue shark is a cosmopolitan species. It is found in the deep waters of the world's oceans, although it avoids colder, polar waters.

RIGHT BOTTOM:
Baitball
This small blue shark has found a good meal on the southern coast of South Africa. It has swum right into the heart of a shoal of anchovies and is eating them from the inside out.

Painful mistake

This bull shark shows some fresh wounds from the bite of another bull shark, which has mistaken it for something a little tastier. In a feeding frenzy, mistakes get made. Sharks go by scent at a distance, and close up their vision is not particularly acute.

LEFT:
Bull shark gang
A magnificent swarm of bull sharks gathers in deep water. Don't be fooled by the grace and beauty – bull sharks are aggressive and most dangerous in shallow waters. They have been known to pursue their victims right to the water's edge.

ABOVE:
Primary weapon
Bull shark jaws are the strongest of all. They have a bite force up to 5914 newtons (1330 lbf), which weight for weight is the highest among all sharks.

Blacktip reef sharks
A common sight in shallow tropical waters near coasts or coral reefs of the Indian Ocean and western Pacific, there are no prizes for guessing where these medium-sized sharks get their name.

ABOVE:
Baby shark
Lemon shark adults return to the same breeding grounds where they started life to produce their young. This species, like most shark species, gives birth to its babies.

OPPOSITE:
Hitch-hikers
Seen from below, this lemon shark appears to have some fellow travellers. Remora fish have a highly modified dorsal fin, which works like a sucker to grip the larger fish's belly. The remora is hauled along by the shark and survives on scraps scavenged from its host's meals.

Snap happy

A lemon shark is caught in action snapping up some bait dangled by shark watchers. The shark will have been lured by the smell. Two-thirds of its brain is designated to processing scent information. It can detect a drop of blood in the water from 1.6km (1 mile) away. That means the shark can still detect the chemicals in the blood even after they are diluted in 2.5km² (1mi²) of water.

Uneasy neighbours
Kayakers share the Hadera Stream with sandbar sharks. This is a small river that meets the Mediterranean on the coast of Israel. Its waters are unnaturally warm due to discharge from a nearby power plant. The sharks come in winter, attracted by the unseasonal heat.

Dusky shark

This medium-sized and slender shark is found in coastal water worldwide. It seldom strays far from the edge of the continental shelf, and instead hunts in the more crowded coastal waters.

Whitetip reef shark
This small shark does not really warrant its name. It is named partly because it lacks the black tip on the dorsal fin seen on blacktip reef shark. The whitetip generally has a pale patch in the corresponding place, but it is seldom bright white. However, there is a white tip to the tail fin.

ABOVE:
Oceanic whitetip
This shark is named for the pale flashes on its dorsal and pectoral fins. It lives worldwide, hunting in the sunlit zone of warm deep waters. However, the whitetip is critically endangered due to an onslaught by the shark fin industry, which catches sharks on a huge scale, and as by-catch in surface nets meant for fish.

OPPOSITE BOTH:
Caribbean reef shark
This medium-sized requiem shark resides in the shallow waters of the western Atlantic. It is most commonly seen around the reefs of the Caribbean, where it lurks in the shadowy water where the reef plunges down into deeper water. The species is currently classified as endangered due to habitat loss.

Baby shark
A baby swell shark hatches from its egg, a tough transulcent case that clings to vegetation on the seabed. Many of the larger galean sharks give birth to their young, but this small species – one of a wider group called cat sharks – lays eggs in common dogfish and bullhead sharks.

Ocean facing
Taking a swim in the ocean, at Bondi Beach as shown here or elsewhere, is very much part of Australian culture. Sharks only attack swimmers if threatened or mistaken, and they largely leave us alone. On average 15 people are attacked in Australian waters each year.

Great white shark

The stuff of nightmares, the white shark is great by name and great by nature. At nearly 6m (20ft) long and weighing in at 2 tonnes, this is the largest hunting fish in the oceans. It is found worldwide but has particular hotspots around Australia, South Africa and the west coast of North America. It could kill a human very easily but very, very seldom does.

LEFT:
Breach attack
The great white attacks from below and to the side, favouring the dark waters of dusk and dawn. It uses its great weight to smash into prey taking an initial bite. It then generally lets go and comes back for a crushing killer bite – if it likes the flavour. The first bite is generally fatal nevertheless. The most violent attacks see the shark surge upwards at such speed that it breaches, or flies out of the water into the air.

ABOVE:
Food supply
Breach attacks are a specialism of South African white sharks, where they gather to feast on the cape fur seals that inhabit the area. The clash of polar and tropical currents that take place around Cape Agulhas at the southern tip of Africa creates a fertile sea and there is plenty to eat for hunter and hunted alike.

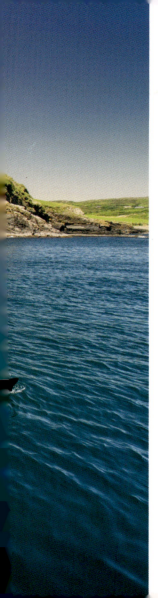

LEFT:
Basking shark
Named after the way this big shark glides along just under or at the surface, as if sunbathing, this is the second-largest fish in the sea. It is harmless to humans and other creatures bigger than its plankton foods. People have been known to travel by standing on the shark's back.

ABOVE:
Open wide
The basking shark eats plankton, which are tiny animals and plant-like algae that float in the seawater. The basking shark swims along with its mouth open wide so water flows into the mouth and out through the gill slits, where plankton is filtered out and swallowed.

ALL PICTURES:
Shortfin mako shark
The term mako is Maori, the indigenous language of New Zealand, for 'shark'. This is one of two species with the name mako, along with the long-fin mako. Both live across the world in warmer waters. Growing to 3m (10ft) long, this species is a fish eater. It uses its tangled hook-like teeth to grip fish and other slippery prey.

ABOVE:
Porbeagle
This medium-sized shark lives in the North Atlantic. Its name is a portmanteau of porpoise and beagle. A long tail fin and rounded, torpedo-shaped body allows this shark to chase down shoaling fish, such as mackerel and herring.

OPPOSITE:
Porbeagle teeth
The teeth of the porbeagle are adapted for spearing fish. The central spike stabs the victim and is locked in place by the smaller spikes either side.

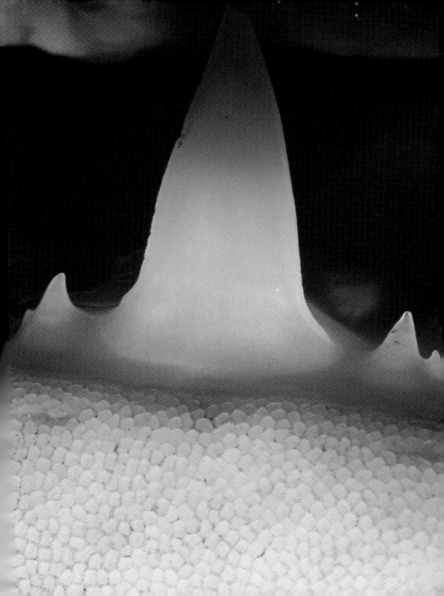

ABOVE TOP AND BOTTOM:
Thresher shark
This widespread fish eater has a highly distinctive upper tail lobe. It uses this long tail to whip the water and stun schooling fish, making it easier for the shark to grab them.

RIGHT:
Goblin shark
This odd-looking shark lives near the seabed in deep water. The pointed snout gets smaller in proportion to the rest of the body as the shark grows. The snout allows the shark's jaws to protrude a long way out of the mouth so that the slow-moving hunter can snap up prey in the dark.

Nurse shark

Despite the name, these sharks are as uncaring as any other species. The term might come from an older word for cat sharks, another type of galean shark, not that closely related. Nurse sharks have two fleshy barbels on the snout, which are used for feeling the seabed. The shark's squared jawline is from a wide mouth that is further forward than that of most sharks, and thus ideal for bottom feeding.

ALL PHOTOGRAPHS:
Tasselled wobbegong

Wobbegong is an Aboriginal word, and these small flattened sharks are found around the coast of Australia, Indonesia and other parts of the western Pacific. They are ambush hunters and highly camouflaged with mottled colouring. This species also use a tangled fringe of hair-like tassels to break up its body shape and blend into the surroundings.

Zebra shark

The bottom-dwelling and nocturnal zebra shark is a predator of shellfish and can grow to 2.5m (8ft) long. It has distinctive ridges down the back and the tail fin has only an upper lobe, which makes up about half the length of the body. The zebra shark can appear to be resting on the seafloor, but it needs a flow of water over the gills to extract oxygen. To this end, the shark chooses a spot where a current is moving a constant supply of water around it.

LEFT:
Zebra shark mouth
What the zebra shark lacks in tooth size is makes up for with numbers. There are about 30 rows of small pointed teeth. The shark uses suction to pull shellfish and other foods into the mouth.

ABOVE:
Spotted skin
Despite the spots of the adult seen here, this carpet shark earns its name when young and the appearance is more patterned like carpet designs. The juvenile form is dark brown with white stripes.

ALL PHOTOGRAPHS:
Whale shark
With more than a passing resemblance to its much smaller carpet shark cousin, this is the largest shark of all. The 19-m (62-ft) monster lives in warmer waters than its distant cousin and fellow filter-feeder, the basking shark, and swims deeper down, ploughing through barely visible blooms of plankton. The pattern of dots on the back is unique to every whale shark.

Aerial view
A whale shark visiting the Sea of Cortez, a narrow inlet of the Pacific in Baja California, Mexico. Whale sharks are a common sight here between July and November.

ALL PHOTOGRAPHS:
Epaulette sharks
These little carpet sharks are named after the large spots behind the pectoral fins, which are reminiscent of the shoulder tags on a military uniform. The fish are also sometimes called long-tail carpet sharks or bamboo sharks, perhaps for their long mottled bodies. They feel for shellfish and other prey in the sediment with their fleshy barbels.

OPPOSITE TOP:
Walking bamboo shark
Yet another name for this small group of fish in the walking shark species because they use their fins to push themselves over the seabed.

OPPOSITE BOTTOM:
Brownbanded bamboo shark
The striped body of this Indonesian species is generally only visible in bright light. In the natural gloom of the seafloor, the stripes help break up the fish's outline so other animals cannot see it.

BELOW:
Hooded epaulette shark
This species of walking shark can be found in the rocky tidal zone surrounding New Guinea and western Indonesia.

Dogfish and Bullhead Sharks

Smaller sharks, about 160 species in all, belong to a group called the Squalomorphii, or squalea. This name is derived from the genus *Squalus*, which contains the most well-known dogfish. These sleek fish look very much like sharks, but are more slender in form and much smaller in length than the typical galean species. They also have a telltale second dorsal fin that is not seen often in the galean sharks. Dogfish sharks occupy the rocky seafloor near to the coast, hunting in the rough water. The dogfish's scientific name also shares its derivation with the term 'squalor', meaning shrouded in filth and darkness. The latter link holds up at least, as many dogfish spend their lives in the deep twilight zones, where light barely reaches. From there vast unseen schools of fish travel up to the surface under cover of night to feed. The dogfish track this great oceanic migration, feasting as they go.

The squalean sharks also include strange members such as angel sharks, which are flatfish that lurk on the seabed, and sawsharks, so named because their long tooth-fringed snouts have the appearance of a wood saw. There are also frilled sharks and cow sharks. These are thought to retain body shapes of primitive species that ruled the seas millions of years ago.

Finally, the bullhead sharks have been included here. Debate continues over whether these small and stout bottom-dwelling sharks are galea or squalea. Their blunt bullish faces are not giving anything away.

OPPOSITE:
Social scene
Sharks are notoriously unfriendly, to each other as much as any other sea creature. However, these Port Jackson sharks, a type of bullhead shark, are often found congregating on the seabed. They tend to be older sharks that do this, gathering with members of the same sex that are of similar size and age.

ALL PHOTOGRAPHS:
Port Jackson shark
This little bottom-dweller is an example of a bullhead shark, so-called because of its robust, large skull. It snuffles through the sediment, using its bottom-facing mouth to crush up shellfish. The shark gets hold of prey by rapidly sucking up sand and water and pumping it out of the gill slits.

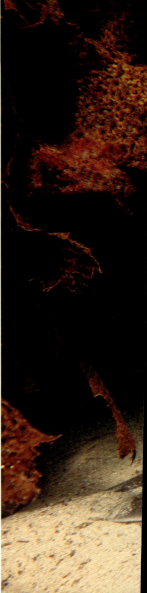

Home sweet home
Port Jackson sharks are named after a stretch of water near Sydney but the small shark (about 1.5m/5ft long) lives around most of the coast of Australia.

RIGHT TOP:
Horn shark
These little sharks from the coast of the Pacific Northwest are named for the spike-like horns that stick out of the dorsal fins.

RIGHT BOTTOM:
Defensive spine
The sharp horn is a defensive weapon. The small shark—it grows to no more than 1 m long—is preyed upon by elephant seals, and the horn makes it a less palatable meal.

OPPOSITE TOP:
Galapagos bullhead
Despite its name, this bullhead shark also lives along the western coast of South America, as well as lurking in the shallows around the Galapagos Islands further out in the Pacific Ocean.

OPPOSITE BOTTOM:
Japanese bullhead
This striped shark lives among the kelp beds around the coasts of the north-west Pacific, which includes the waters of Korea and China as well as Japan.

Hidden egg
The horn shark lays heavily disguised eggs in thick seaweed. The green egg case has a lustre that matches the slimy fronds of the kelp around it.

Sawsharks

This amazing group of sharks obviously get their name from the way their teeth stick out the side of an elongated bony snout, creating the look of an old-fashioned saw. There are ten sawshark species living in the sheltered tropical waters of the Indian and Pacific oceans. This Bahamian species is the only Atlantic species.

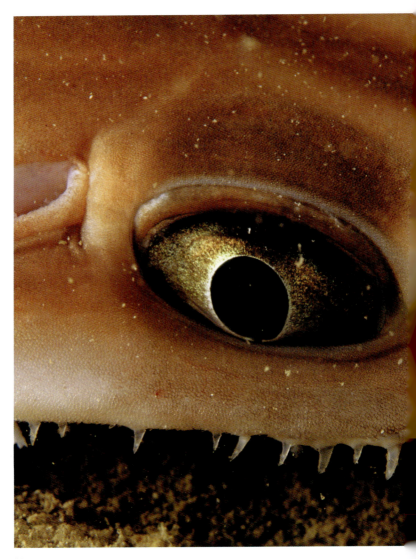

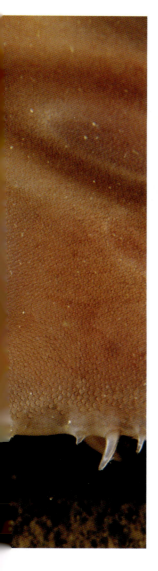

ALL PHOTOGRAPHS:
Longnose sawshark
This sawshark is aptly named in that its toothy rostrum makes up a third of its total body length. The fish lives in the waters south of Australia. It uses the two long barbels poking from the snout to detect buried prey. The sawshark uses the toothed 'saw' as a digging implement to stir up the sediment and then snap up worms and other prey in its downward-facing mouth.

OPPOSITE TOP:
Brier shark
This deepwater dogfish lives worldwide and searches for prey on the seabed. It is also called a birdbeak shark.

OPPOSITE BOTTOM:
Prickly dogfish
This strange fish has extremely rough skin and a distinctive hump on its back. The fish lives around Australia and New Zealand, swimming in the dark waters of the continental slope where the seabed falls away to the deepest areas of the ocean.

ABOVE:
Spiny dogfish
Also called a spurdog or mud shark, this small shark lives in the colder coastal waters of every continent. It preys on fish and other swimming prey, and is known to hunt in packs in their thousands.

Greenland shark

This sluggish deep-sea hunter lives in cold Arctic waters. Seldom seen at the surface, it is thought to be the longest-living vertebrate of all, with some reaching an age of 500 years. The Greenland shark is also one of the biggest fish, easily as long as fearsome hunters such as bull sharks and tiger sharks. It too is a hunter, but it targets smaller fish in slow-motion strikes.

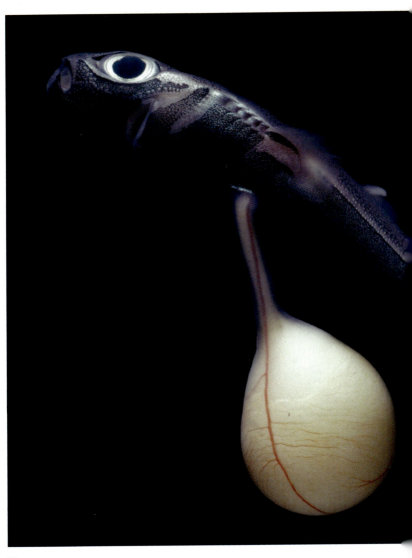

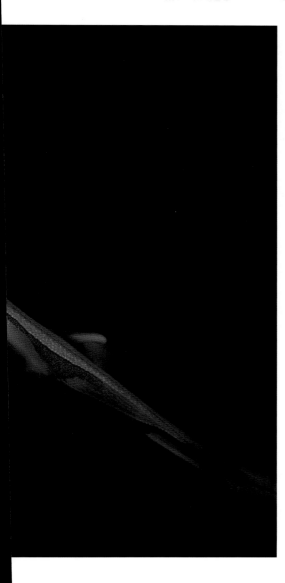

LEFT:
Newborn shark
This baby spined pygmy shark has just been born. It is too small to fend for itself and so is being sustained by a yolk sac. This is a bag of food and nutrients that developed alongside the embryo inside the mother.

OVERLEAF:
Spined pygmy shark
This is one of the smallest sharks. It grows to just 22cm (8in).
The species lives in the twilight zone around continental slopes.
Here they prey on vast shoals of lanternfish that migrate up and down in the water column.

ABOVE TOP AND BOTTOM:
Pacific angelshark
The angelsharks are ambush predators that lie flat on the seabed. This species lives along the western coast of North and South America. It eyes face upwards so it can see prey as they swim overhead. When a target fish or squid comes close enough, the shark will strike.

RIGHT:
Japanese angelshark
This species lives on sandy areas of the seabed around the Sea of Japan and northern Pacific. It grows to about 1.5m (5ft) long. It is critically endangered because of being targeted by fishermen, who sell the skin for use as leather and finishing paper for woodworking.

LEFT AND OVERLEAF:
Broadnose sevengill shark
This is a member of the cow shark group, which mostly have six gill slits, not the usual five for other kinds of shark. As the name suggests, this species has one extra slit on top of that. The 2-m (6.5-ft) shark preys on seals and large fish – including other sharks. It lives mostly in the coastal areas of the Southern Hemisphere, favouring regions that are fed by cold oceanic currents.

LEFT AND OVERLEAF:
Frill shark
This animal has been around for millions more years than most shark species and it is described as a 'living fossil'. The 2m (6.5 ft) shark lacks the usual sleek finned body, but has retained a primitive eel-shaped form instead. The shark is named after its large and flexible gill slits. It also has a tangle of hooked teeth for gripping prey.

Six-gill shark

As the name suggests, this species is typical of cow sharks in that it has six gill slits. Despite looking similar to other galean sharks, the cow sharks are thought to be closer in form to ancient sharks, like their relative the frilled sharks.

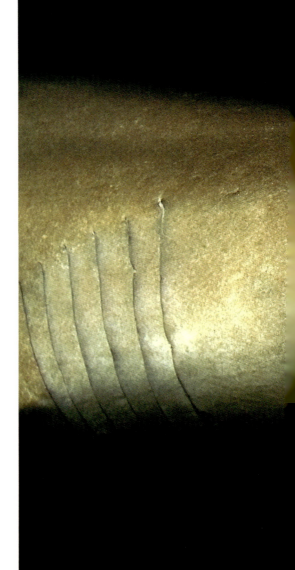

Rays and Skates

A defining feature of sharks is their skeletons. Instead of bone, these internal frameworks are made from cartilage. This feature is shared with a sister group called the Batoidea, which are more commonly known as rays and skates. All batoids are flatfish that are squashed from top to bottom, making a rounded body with a long, slender tail trailing behind. The pectoral fins form large wing-like lobes that make up most of the bodies of rays and skates. The head is subsumed by the lobes, so the eyes peer out the top and the mouth is largely hidden from view, facing the seabed.

This body shape is indicative of a life spent on or close to the seafloor. The wing-shaped fins allow the fish to make short glides over the sand and mud, before nestling into the sediment to avoid further attention. Some rays, including the largest and most majestic – the manta rays – have switched to a life swimming in the sunlit zones of the open ocean. In this case, the fins have become water wings, and the manta ray swims with gentle flaps of its fins.

The 600-odd species of ray divide into three major orders. Rajiformes are the skates, perhaps confusingly. They swim with a typical undulating frill of the fins and lack a sting in the tail. The Myliobatiformes by contrast are sting rays, although not all, such as the mantas, have stingers. The stingers are thorn-like spikes that are delivered with a flick of the tail and become lodged in the target's flesh. The other main ray order are the Torpediniformes, or electric rays. These medium-sized fish can deliver a nasty shock.

OPPOSITE:
Bluespotted ribbontail ray
The colourful markings on this timid reef-living ray are there as a warning. The slender flexible tail is tipped with stingers that lodge in the skin and create excruciating – but not fatal – injuries.

Spiracle

While sharks (and most other fish) 'breathe' in water through the mouth, rays draw water in through a spiracle located by each eye. The water entering here passes through the gills and out of slits on the underside of the ray.

Devil rays

These relatives of the manta rays are known for breaching the surface and gliding a short distance on their wing-like fins. Rays take the air when they gather in large shoals, but no one really understands why.

ALL PHOTOGRAPHS:
Mass meeting
The largest groups of devil rays gather on the Pacific coast of Mexico. The rays are filter feeders and here they are following swarms of tiny shrimp-like plankton.

LEFT:

Marbled torpedo ray
The underside of a ray is not often on show. This torpedo ray's mouth and gills are located on its underside. Rays are flattened top to bottom so that they are less conspicuous when patrolling on or close to the seabed. However, manta rays and other species have adapted to life swimming nearer the surface.

ABOVE:

Electric rays
Electric rays, or torpedoes, can be differentiated from other rays by their shark-like tail fins. Electric organs along each side of the ray's body deliver a large electric shock to anything that touches their back or belly. The fish uses this weapon to stun fish around it, or ward off attack. The charge can be strong enough to kill a human.

Hidden danger
A gulf torpedo relies on a mottled texture on its back to help it blend into the sandy seabed of the Red Sea, Persian Gulf and coastal waters around the Indian Ocean.

ALL PHOTOGRAPHS AND OVERLEAF:

Giant oceanic manta ray
This is the largest species of ray. Its wing-like fins are 7m (23ft) wide, and thanks to the tail spike, the fish is 9m (30ft) long. Manta rays have distinctive cephalic fins under the eye and either side of the mouth. These are rolled up while swimming and unfurled to funnel water into the mouth when the fish is filtering out plankton foods.

Cleaning station
This reef manta ray has just visited a cleaning station where smaller fish pick off the parasites and specks of dirt on the bigger fish's flat body.

Harmless giant
The manta ray's long tail is flexible but trails out behind its expansive flattened body much of the time. There are no stingers or pointed spines on the tip.

OPPOSITE, LEFT TOP AND MIDDLE:
Short-tail stingray
This sturdy ray lives in the waters around South Africa, southern Australia and New Zealand. As the name suggests, the thick tail is shorter than the rest of the body.

LEFT BOTTOM:
Soft skin
The short-tail stingray is also called the smooth stingray because the tooth-like denticles that cover the skins of most sharks and rays are only present on its tail. The rest of the body is smoother to the touch.

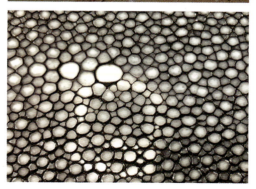

ALL PHOTOGRAPHS:
Thornback ray
This ray, also known as a thornback skate, is found in the coastal waters of the eastern Atlantic and western parts of the Indian Ocean. As its name suggests, the back is covered in prominent spines. Older females also grow these protective features on their undersides.

OVERLEAF:
Down-turned face
The thornback ray is a bottom feeder. It sucks up shrimps, crabs, worms and other sea life that lives on or in seabed sediment. The mouth has many small teeth for crushing and grinding food.

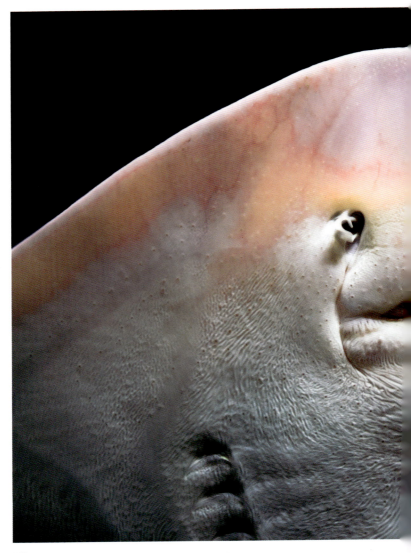

Big skate
Perhaps unimaginatively named, this Pacific coastal species is the largest ray species in North American waters. The bottom feeder, which scours the mud for scallops, grows to 2m (6.5ft) long.

OPPOSITE TOP:
Dead eye
This is the remains of a big skate that washed up on a beach in Washington State, USA.

OPPOSITE BOTTOM:
Looking up
In common with other bottom feeders, the eyes of the big skate are on top of the head and look upwards. They search for shadows overhead that might represent threats. Additionally, the spiracles allow the fish to keep breathing when largely buried in sediment.

ABOVE:
In deep water
This pointy-faced skate was photographed around one kilometre under the water.

Little snake
This ray found swimming in open water along the east coast of North America is only about 40cm (15.5in) wide. It moves in a punting motion by pushing off the seabed using spines near the base of its tail, so that the fish glides forward a little before landing again.

OPPOSITE TOP AND BOTTOM:
Small eyes and a big mouth
The little snake spends the days buried in sediment and emerges at night to feed. It only has small eyes and relies more on its electrical sensors to find prey and mates. The little ray feeds mostly on worms and crustaceans that are buried in the seabed sediment.

ABOVE:
Thorny skate
This rough-back fish is covered, as its name suggests, in many small thorns. It prefers colder waters in the North Atlantic and so is often found living deep down. This one was found in shallower waters off the coast of Greenland.

LEFT AND OVERLEAF:
Undulate ray
Preferring the shallower waters of the Eastern Atlantic, this species is found all the way from the equator to the British Isles. It is an easy catch and as a result is now classified as vulnerable due to overfishing.

Other Predators

The ocean is a habitat in which it is easy to be a predator and there are plenty of them about. This may seem counter-intuitive to those familiar with food chains and food webs. Nearly all food webs begin with plants that harvest the energy in sunlight. This energy is passed on through a chain of animals that eat the plants and then each other. On land, it is a simple fact that the amount of plant material vastly outweighs the number of animals, and the plant-eating animals in turn outweigh the predators. Think of the vast herds of wildebeest on the African plain, and the small gangs of lions. This arrangement, however, is turned on its head in the oceans. There the producers are not trees or grasses but phytoplankton, microscopic photosynthesizers that, nevertheless, do the same job equally as well. Yet, these short-lived, plant-like organisms add up to less biomass than the ocean grazers that feed upon them. These are creatures such as krill and other zooplankton. The zooplankton make up the bulk of marine biomass, which means there is a lot of food out there for ocean predators, from jellyfish to real fish, from cunning octopuses to brutal mantis shrimps, and everything else in between. This chapter focuses on the non-mammal ocean hunters. Most of them are seldom seen, being too small or existing too deep down, but they still pack quite a punch.

OPPOSITE:
Jellyfish
Often tiny and too translucent to see, jellyfish are among the simplest of ocean predators. Combined these diffuse creatures add up to double the mass of the world's humans and 20 times the mass of wild mammals on land and in the sea.

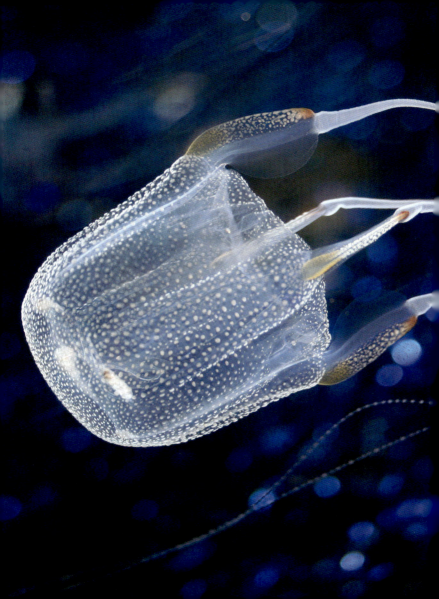

Sea wasp
Also called box jellyfish due to their vaguely quadrilateral shape, these little jellyfish produce a painful but ultimately harmless sting. They use their stinger tentacles to collect small planktonic crustaceans.

ABOVE:
Dangerous to know
Some box jellyfish are highly venomous, and can kill humans. The best treatment for a jellyfish sting is vinegar or another weak acid that stops the stinger cells from activating.

RIGHT:
Round bodies
Jellyfish and their kin belong to a distinct sub-kingdom of animals called the Radiata. They have round bodies with no distinct front or back. They don't have a mouth or anus, just a single central opening that does both jobs at once.

Great barracuda
With a mean mouth packed full of teeth, this hunting fish gets its prey using an ambush technique. It lurks in the shadows and then surges into view at speeds of 40km/h (25mph) to snap up smaller fish.

Lionfish

This fish is named after the mane-like spines that surround the head. Several of the long spines on the back can deliver a powerful venom. The spines deter attackers and are also used to catch prey. The venom is powerful enough to kill a human, although fatal stings are rare.

LEFT:
Slow-motion killer
The lionfish is slow but deadly. It eats other small fish. They squirt jets of water at their victim, forcing it into a corner. The spines then fan out blocking any escape and the lionfish eats its victim head first.

ABOVE:
Striped warning
The striped colouring of the lionfish helps the body merge with the spine making the fish look much larger than it really is.

Sarcastic fringehead
The strangely named Pacific blenny also has a strange lifestyle. It lurks in rocky crevices and wants to be left alone. When another sarcastic fringehead passes by, it rushes out with its large mouth spread open wide. The two fish then lock mouths as if kissing and have a battle of strength to decide who rules the territory.

ALL PHOTOGRAPHS:
Scorpionfish
These relatives of the lionfish also have venomous spines along their backs. Many of them live on the rocky seabed where they blend in with their surroundings. These fish produce lots of venom, and will pump it into the foot of an unsuspecting paddler. However, the toxins are neutralized by being soaked in warm water.

Sailfish
Despite its appearance, the sail of this hunting fish is not used to catch the wind. Instead, it is flapped up and down using flexible spines as a way of communicating with and confusing prey.

OPPOSITE:
High speed
Sailfish are among the fastest fish in the sea, along with similar swordfish and marlin. It can hit a speed of 110km/h (68mph), which is fast enough to make great leaps into the air.

ABOVE:
Fish baiting
A sailfish herds its prey into a tight shoal and then slashes at them using its sword-shaped snout. That stuns a number of fish for the hunter to then snap up.

ALL PHOTOGRAPHS:
Sea anemones
Instead of floating in the water with their sting-covered tentacles hanging down, sea anemones – relatives of jellyfish – sit on the seabed upside down. Their tentacles are covered in millions of tiny stinger cells that work together to grab any animals that come within reach, including this butterfly fish.

OPPOSITE:
Jelly battle
Pale white anemones feast on a swarm of Mastigias jellyfish. These sea anemones in the estuary of the St Lawrence River were waiting for one meal when hundreds arrived all at once.

ABOVE:
Tentacles
The tentacles sift food from the water and transport it to the anemone's mouth, which is located in the middle of the body.

BELOW:
Colourful killer
This species is a pink violet anemone. Despite sharing its name with a flower, the sea anemone is very much an animal.

OPPOSITE:
Family in residence
Clownfish are immune to the stings of the anemone. They have a layer of slick mucus that stops the stingers from hitting home. The fish keep the anemone clean and the anemone provides the fish with a fortress to live in safe from attack.

Tuna
A large shoal of tuna swims through the Mediterranean Sea. These big fish hunt in groups and use their speed to chase down smaller fish.

Yellowfin tuna

Named for is shiny gold colouring, this tuna fish is found worldwide and is considerably larger than the skipjack and bluefin tuna. At 400kg (880lbs) and 2.5m (8ft) long, it is one of the biggest tuna species.

ALL PHOTOGRAPHS:
Blue-ringed octopus
Do not be fooled by the beauty of this small octopus found in the coastal seas of Pacific and Indian Ocean. The blue rings throb invitingly but this is a warning to watch out. One bite from this golf ball-sized mollusc will kill a person in minutes.

Greater blue-ringed octopus

This is one of several blue-ringed octopus species. Despite its name, it is not larger than the lesser blue-ringed octopus. The species are so named because of the size of their blue rings.

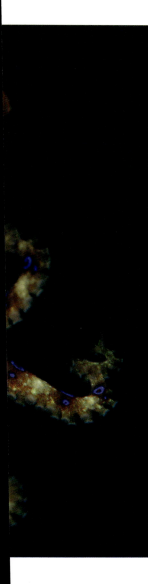

ALL PHOTOGRAPHS:
The deadliest venom
The blue-ringed octopus's venom contains tetrodotoxin, the most potent toxin produced by animals. The poison is actually made by symbiotic bacteria.

OVERLEAF:
Day octopus
This day octopus has just snagged a squid. Living on the coral reefs of the Pacific and Indian oceans, it is so named because it hunts during daylight hours. This is unusual for octopods, which tend to be nocturnal.

Pacific giant octopus
This giant Pacific octopus is eating a dogfish and is not happy at being disturbed. Octopuses and other cephalopods are well known for the way they can change colour. They do this using coloured cells in the skin that expand and contract to mix colours, in a system not dissimilar to a television screen. Colour changes help with camouflage but also display mood.

Pacific giant octopus
At more than 4m (13ft) long, the giant Pacific octopus is the largest octopus species in the world. They live to be about four years old, with both males and females dying soon after breeding.

OPPOSITE:
Night crawler
The giant Pacific octopus is active at night. It passes the day in a rocky refuge away from prying eyes. As darkness falls, it spends most of its time on the seabed in search of shellfish to eat.

LEFT TOP:
Convergent evolution
The cephalopod eye is similar in its gross anatomy to the human eye and it works in much the same way. This is a great example of convergent evolution whereby natural selection creates the same adaptation more than once. If anything the octopus's eye is better than ours because there is no blind spot.

LEFT MIDDLE AND BOTTOM:
Capture system
The octopus grabs prey with its powerful suckers. Its central nervous system spreads into the eight arms. In many ways the whole body is largely brain.

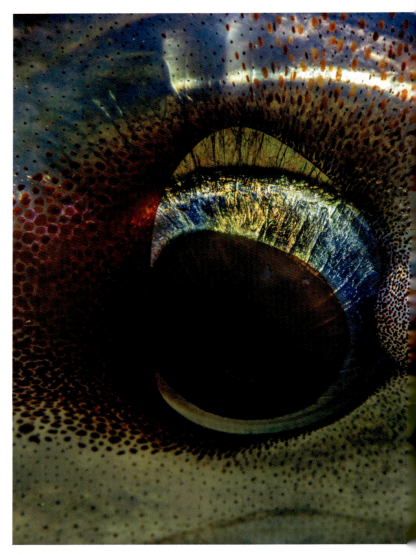

ALL PHOTOGRAPHS:
Bigfin reef squid
This beautifully coloured species, which ranges from the eastern Mediterranean to Australia, is one of the main commercial species. When we eat calamari, it might well be one of these.

Reflective layer

This bigfin reef squid is out swimming at a reef in Bali during the middle of night. This species of squid is able to change the colour of its skin very rapidly. It is also very unusual in that it is able to turn on structures in the skin that reflect ambient light.

LEFT:
Humboldt squid
The Humboldt is a big squid that rises up to hunt nearer the surface at night. The largest squid are illusive deep sea creatures that have almost never been caught on camera. This image shows the siphon (below centre), a nozzle that the squid uses to propel itself along with jets of water.

ABOVE:
Cannibal
The Humboldt squid has one behaviour in common with most other squid – they are cannibals. The squid on the left seems to be winning in the battle to eat.

ABOVE:
European spider crab
This species of crab has exceptionally long legs and resembles a spider hence its name (not to be confused with crab spiders). The European spider crab is much smaller than the Japanese species, which can be 3m (10ft) wide.

RIGHT:
European edible crab
As the name suggests, this is the species that graces dining tables. Most crabs are predators but they sit in the middle of ocean food webs and so are also prey themselves.

ABOVE:

Sargassum swimming crab

This free-swimming crab has snared a baby squid. It lives on the floating seaweeds that give the Sargasso Sea in the central Atlantic its name.

RIGHT:

Coconut crabs

This species of terrestrial hermit crab is from the coast of Tanzania. Some of the largest crabs live on land and only return to the water to breed.

ALL PHOTOGRAPHS:
American lobster
The lobster is a ten-legged relative of crabs and shrimps. The fifth set of legs are the pincers, which are not used for walking but for grabbing prey and ripping it to pieces.

LEFT:
Touch and sniff
Lobsters rely heavily on their sense of touch and smell. The former sense is centred on a long pair of antennae, whereas the latter sense is picked up by smaller antennae in between the feelers.

ABOVE:
Common spiny lobster
This kind of lobster lacks the pincers of true lobsters. The other big difference is that the antennae are very sturdy and covered in spines.

ABOVE:
Protecting eggs
A peacock mantis shrimp protects its eggs in a hollow in the nest. The female produces one ball of eggs for her and the other for the father to look after.

RIGHT:
Mantis shrimp
These large seafloor crustaceans are named after the way their front legs flick out at great speed to grab prey. There are spearers and smashers.

Amazing eyes

The mantis shrimp's eyes are among the best in the animal kingdom. They are able to pick up at least 12 different colours, unlike the three that human eyes detect.

Marine Mammal Hunters

It would seem that sharks have some rivals in the battle to rule the oceans. Whereas sharks have been patrolling the oceans for 400 million years, the mammals returned to ocean life barely 50 million years ago. The pinnipeds, otherwise known as seals and sea lions, belong with big cats, bears and wolves as members of the Carnivora order. This is the top team of predators among mammals, and while pinnipeds are almost helpless out of water, they are deathly effective in it. Other mammal carnivores have adopted a marine life, most notably the polar bear. Often said to be the largest land hunter on Earth, this beast is mostly found at sea.

Whales and dolphins are relatives of hoofed beasts, such as cattle and camels, but have nevertheless taken on the job of being the largest animals in the sea – and the smartest, too. The toothed whales, which includes dolphins and porpoises, are all predators. The killer whale, or orca, is in effect a very big dolphin – and a very deadly one. Anyone who has ever wondered who would win in a battle between an orca and a great white shark need not wonder long. The killer whale lacks the surgical sharp teeth of a shark, but they don't need them. The bite strength of that squared-off mammalian jaw simply crushes any foe. Adult great whites are a rare delicacy for deep-water orcas. They flip the fish onto its back, rendering it helpless. Whales tend to only eat the shark's oily liver, like a cetacean Hannibal Lecter. They leave the rest for the ocean scavengers.

OPPOSITE:
Antarctic fur seal
This baby fur seal is coming to the end of its first summer on a sub-Antarctic Island and will soon set off out to sea to hunt for fish all winter. Also called a sea lion, fur seals are easy to spot by their little external ears and long front flippers.

ALL PHOTOGRAPHS:
Southern elephant seals
A pair of bull seals fight it out to win control of a breeding territory and become the beach master. Elephant seals are the largest kind of seal in the world, although the males are at least twice the size of the females. Like all seals, these animals have short front flippers and no outer ears.

ALL PHOTOGRAPHS:
California sea lions
These Pacific hunters patrol coastal waters and will spend weeks out at sea in the winter. They eat fish and squid and use their whiskers (below) to track the water currents left by these small animals. They can zero in on prey in pitch dark water. Sea lions are themselves prey for orcas and sharks.

LEFT:
Walrus
These huge sea mammals are bottom feeders. They plunge to the seabed and snuffle about. They use their impressive moustaches to feel for shellfish and other foods buried in the sediment.

ABOVE:
Breeding colony
Thousands of walruses gather on Alaskan beaches. As sea ice cover drops due to global warming, walruses are finding it harder to find places to rest between feeds.

LEFT:
Eurasian otter
This otter has caught a crab. Although it also hunts in rivers, the otter can be found along beaches and around river mouths. In some parts of Europe, the animal is known as a sea cat.

ABOVE BOTH PHOTOGRAPHS:
Polar bears
The polar bear is a marine animal. It spends most of its life at sea, albeit a frozen one, as it sniffs out seals swimming below the ice. The bear can swim for long distances using its wide, webbed paws as paddles.

Sea bear
The scientific name for polar bears is Thalarctos maritimus, which means 'northern sea bear.' Because of expected habitat loss caused by climate change, the polar bear is classified as a vulnerable species.

Killer whales

Three orcas, or killer whales, spy-hop through a hole in the ice. They do this to take a look around above the water. Hunting techniques are passed down through generations, so their diets depend on the region they inhabit and the pod's approach to hunting.

Sperm whale

At 16m (52ft) long, the sperm whale is the largest hunter on Earth. This toothed whale, a distant relative of dolphins, hunts out of sight deep down in waters where no sunlight reaches. Whales use sonar calls focused through a ball of oil and gel in their rounded snouts. That system is used for tracking down another sea monster: the giant squid. Sperm whales often have scars and scratches inflicted by the beaks of their prey as they fight it out in the deep.

LEFT:
Common dolphin
A pair of common dolphins work together to grab sardines. The waters of South Africa are filled with billions of these fish every winter, which attract dolphins, sharks and many other ocean hunters.

ABOVE:
Bottlenose dolphins
A pair of bottlenose dolphins head off to new hunting grounds. This most familiar of dolphin species is found in warm oceans worldwide.

Credits

Alamy: 11 (Jeff Rotman), 22/23 (Media Drum World), 36/37 & 38 (Stocktrek Images, Inc), 40/41 (Mark Conlin), 48 (Cultura Creative RF), 49 (Nature Picture Library), 50 (Nature Picture Library), 52 (Doug Perrine), 53 (Doug Perrine), 54 top (Nature Picture Library), 55 (Marko Steffensen), 58 (WaterFrame), 60/61 (SeaTops), 62 (Biosphoto), 68 top (Jeff Rotman), 68 bottom (Christian Loader), 70 top (Stocktrek Images, Inc), 70 bottom (Jane Gould), 71 top (Jeff Rotman), 71 bottom (Blue Planet Archive), 72 (Auscape International Pty Ltd), 74 top (Biosphoto), 74 bottom (Jeff Rotman), 76/77 (David Fleetham), 78 top (Mark Conlin/VWPics), 78 bottom (Mark Conlin), 79 top (tbkmedia.de), 80/81 (Mark Conlin/VWPics), 84 & 85 (Auscape International Pty Ltd), 86 top & bottom (Kelvin Aitken/VWPics), 88/89 (louise murray), 90/91 (Jeff Rotman), 92/93 (Jeff Rotman), 94 top (Nature Picture Library), 94 bottom (Helmut Corneli), 95 (Kelvin Aitken/VWPics), 102/103 (mauritius images GmbH), 115 (imageBroker), 118 bottom (Hans Gert Broeder), 119 (Cultura Creative RF), 120/121 (Nature Picture Library), 126 (WaterFrame), 127 top (F1online digitale Bildagentur GmbH), 132/133 (David Fleetham), 134 top (Lee Rentz), 135 (Kelvin Aitken/VWPics), 136/137 & 138 both (Jeff Rotman), 139 & 140/141 (Poelzer Wolfgang), 142/143 (Biosphoto), 144 (Gino's Premium Images), 146/147 (Sabena Jane Blackbird), 148 (WorldFoto), 159 (Cigdem-Sean Cooper), 164 top (mauritius images GmbH), 164 bottom (Jeff Rotman), 166 (WaterFrame), 169 (Stocktrek Images, Inc.), 174 (Reinhard Dirscherl), 175 (imageBroker), 180/181 (Ethan Daniels), 182/183 (Minden Pictures), 186 (David Fleetham), 187 bottom (Jeff Rotman), 192 (WaterFrame), 193-195 (WaterFrame), 196 (Blue Planet Archive), 197 (Gary Roberts), 211 (Nick Polanszky), 218/219 (Ralph Lee Hopkins), 222 (Cultura Creative Ltd)

Dreamstime: 13 (Matthew Mcclure), 16 (Marmite07), 46 (Sergey Uryadnikov), 56/57 (Pniesen), 75 (Irko Van Der Heide), 114 (Mark Doherty), 176/177 (Pics516), 179 (Erika Antoniazzo), 203 (Kjersti Joergensen), 212 (Lukas Blazek), 220/221 (Martin Procházka)

Getty Images: 17 (Richard Bouhet/AFP), 30/31 (Reinhard Dirscherl), 66/67 (Guillermo Arias/AFP), 100/101 (Awashima Marine Park), 160/161 (Reinhard Dirscherl/ullstein bild)

Shutterstock: 5 (Narchuk), 6 (Thierry Eidenweil), 7 (Shane Myers Photography), 8 (Edgar Photosapiens), 10 (Tomas Kotouc), 12 (wildestanimal), 14/15 (Matt9122), 18/19 (Julian Gunther), 20 (Guillermo Cervetto), 21 top (Samy Kassem), 21 bottom (Alessandro De Maddalena), 24 (Vladimir Turkenich), 25 (lego 19861111), 26/27 (Yann hubert), 28 (Agami Photo Agency), 29 (Fiona Ayerst), 32/33 (Luciano Santandreu), 34/35 (ilan elgrably), 39 top (Jesus Cobaleda), 39 bottom (Tomas Kotouc), 42/43 (365 Focus Photography), 44/45 (Martin Prochazkacz), 47 (Ethan Daniels), 51 (Alessandro De Maddalena), 54 bottom (Shane Gross), 59 top (DiveIvanov), 59 bottom (Ethan Daniels), 63 (aquapix), 64 (Coral Brunner), 65 (SaltedLife), 69 (Ethan Daniels), 79 bottom (tank200bar), 82/83 (Arzi), 87 (Boris Pamikov), 96/97 (wildestanimal), 98/99 (Tomas Kotouc), 104/105 (Greg Amptman), 106 (Swen Andreas Becht), 108/109 (Gialdini Luca), 110/111 (Sergey Uryadnikov), 112 (Dino Adventure), 113 (Hannes Klostermann), 116/117 (yeshaya dinerstein), 118 top (cineuno), 122/123 & 124/125 (Subphoto.com), 127 middle (katherineobrien), 127 bottom (mummyz), 128/129 (MattiaATH), 130/131 (kirpad), 134 bottom (Greg Amptman), 149 (Dr. Victor Wong), 150/151 (Rich Carey), 152/153 (Laura Dts), 154 (fenkieandreas), 155 (Jenny Lord), 156/157 (Greg Amptman), 158 (Richard Whitcombe), 162 (kelldallfall), 163 (Image Source Trading Ltd), 165 (Ethan Daniels), 167 (RLS Photo), 168 (Andrea Izzotti), 170/171 (Guido Montaldo), 172/173 (Jsegalexplore), 178 (Oksana Maksymova), 184/185 (Kondratuk Aleksei), 187 top (Mike Workman), 187 middle (Conchi Martinez), 188 & 189 top (Osman Temizel), 189 bottom & 190/191 (DiveIvanov), 198-199 (RLS Photo), 200 (Gerald Robert Fischer), 201 (Vladimir Wrangel), 202 (Timothy Baxter), 204/205 (John A. Anderson), 206 (Tarpan), 208 (Jeremy Richards), 209 top (Dennis Stogsdill), 209 bottom (Randy Runtsch), 210 top (Finn Steiner), 210 bottom (Chelsea Cameron), 213 (Hal Brindley), 214 (Karl Weller), 215 top (Christopher Wood), 215 bottom (GTW), 216/217 (Michael Cola), 223 (Pikkymaster)